THE FUTURE OF LOVE

john poch

THE FUTURE OF LOVE

poems

SL/.NT
BOOKS

THE FUTURE OF LOVE
Poems

Slant Books
P.O. Box 60295
Seattle, WA 98160

www.slantbooks.org

Cataloguing-in-Publication data:

Names: Poch, John.

Title: The future of love: poems / John Poch.

Description: Seattle, WA: Slant Books, 2025

Identifiers: ISBN 978-1-63982-212-6 (hardcover) | ISBN 978-1-63982-211-9 (paperback) | ISBN 978-1-63982-213-3 (ebook)

Subjects: LCSH: Poetry | American poetry | Love poetry, English | Spain—Poetry

Contents

III

For Meghan, again

I

And in which darkness it can best be proved.

—Eavan Boland

PLEASE

The difference between a glass
of sunlight and your throat
in water is not so simple. Hollows.

Keep your hair up all day
so I can pretend I'm at the ocean.

If you could unroll
the fingers of my hand
from its fist of hardship,
you would see a map of lines,
or a tough palm and tougher prints
destined for turning Bible paper
late night by lamplight.
You might sense cinnamon.
Sugar in the cut wood of juniper.

Like a child enamored
with a tangerine,
I lose myself
peeling the rind away
in one slow whole,
forgetting the present.

This may be a fault, but this is
how I love your clothes.

THE THREAD

The first song in the city this summer of my return
is the cry of a drill grinding a hole through
a marble wall, and that is the sound of flamenco,
a rusted knife on bone, a thief of hours crying
over spilled sherry his news of a lost love lost
for good, for the good in a deep song, the sound
of a coin in the mouth of the dead, carried by
a wind poured out like a pretty little fountain
of whitest feathers dangling from a stork's breast.

My old haunt, Sevilla, you dark lady, sticky flowers
in your hair and fresh scuffs on the shine of your shoes,
your outlandish dress and your barrettes strewn
like you meant it or didn't mean it, we'll never know.
I nearly no longer need a map until the tangle
of narrow streets of Santa Cruz has me lost again
and thrown somehow into derelict Macarena
when I was trying to reach the blessèd river.

This seeming disappointment is the amazement
after making love, your buildings' crumbling
plaster dust dropping its dull incense on me
and the beloved evidence of my own passage.
The beautiful letdown of the lost waiting
to be found might be the scent of citrus flowers.
In this city, the river is not a river, and no one cares
which way or if the weather vane works.

In our oldest plaza, a green parrot struggles to fly
and carry into sky one shred, this long thread torn
from a fallen date palm branch and borne toward
the high green alcove where she will weave a nest.
Into the palm the small burden is lifted up and up
to make a home in blinding heaven out of longing.

FLAMENCO

If you come, bring your best edge sharpened
but hidden on your thigh. I'll guess and watch
your tendency to strum with your thumb
held on the top string holding that chord you love
that always makes wide gray water appear
in the mind, or plains of bleached grain
far from wide water. Among delicate yet
strong scratches do that sad tap as sure
as my name is yours. Your name is not a title,
but I want to read the penultimate page
of your white waves and resist the turn to the last.
Make me last well into the future of ink silence.
I find my reflection in the bottom of your well.
If you truly are the daughter of a red line
of butchers, bring your care for the bleeding pinks
of flamingos. You click your fingers at your tongue
and your tongue clicks back, and your heels,
and we rise for your clapping like a horse
is coming. Why do I long for the horse
the color of coffee mixed with night rain,
the black strength of a wet brown flank?
Go ahead and stab the ripe pomegranate
with a bronze spear twice your height.
We all long for the great bull roaming the hills
to collapse at your feet and the lion of grief
to come and lick your toes because you
have become the green smell of the purple
and fallen jacaranda blossom, O good grief.

GRANADA

This evening, the swallows are getting even
against the gravity of mortal siesta. Between
the earth and sky, they swirl above the Albaicín
like detritus in a sink draining, the ash and butts
of cigarettes, but with razor wings of rushing
and high-pitched trembling little police whistles
of urgency and emergency erasing the quiet.
Despite the city's filth below, the olives
on your plate up here on this high terrace
taste of oregano, cumin, and a clean green kitchen
strangely on the left back fat of your tongue so you want
to sing some slow song of pain. But you don't
know how. Remember Friday's midnight stroll
down the mostly abandoned carnival midway
after you let go a week's reading and drudgery?
You watched some innocent American teen
on the giant boat ride against the sky lose her shoe
while her friends lost their senses, laughing till
they cried and crying till they laughed. You loved them
for how they could let go.
Now the sky darkens, lets go
its pinks to flamingo, its flamingo to flamenco,
rich, then an absence of day as black as a hole
in a guitar. God alone has the victory. We, my love,
the people of the book, war and win by losing because
someone will always need salvation's essence and repetition
even in graffiti that screams from a punk, needy,
unemployed, in love with a girl who hates him
high on paint fumes, scrawling: God, I love graffiti!
and her name nine times in letters the size of her body
on the walls off the tracks of one station outside the city:
KATE KATE KATE KATE KATE KATE KATE KATE KATE

ENTRE DOS AGUAS

Between the perfection of the Biblical seven
and Dante's nine, you lie there in the sheets,
the lithest sepia late-eighteenth-century eight
in the Archive of the Indies, the hand curved
on laid cotton in some fertile praise of the Mississippi
from one honorable servant of the governor.
You govern color, the fuchsia bougainvillea,
the pink, the orange of dying fire all hung over
my morning walk like new dresses teasing
the ravishing girls to give up their studies and run.

Your figure is classic as the study of a pedestal,
as the anchor rung into song by its own chain.
Here, brown skeins of seaweed wait in the wind
like the hair of the saddest waitress in Andalucía.
Drowsy among the shadows of the orange trees
in the shadow of the abandoned castle
in the shadow of the cathedral and her tower,
she tips her cigarette into siesta's oblivion.
Her infinite motto: *No me ha dejado.*

Your hair is the color of the buff rust swallows' bellies
banking above the river after four days of rain.
They fill the air and, by the sun setting on gentle water,
are lit from below that color, chattering
and scissoring the light into confettied money, banking.

If you are the book wise photographers read
to understand the shadow and whet the line,
I am less than a chunk of broken concrete, and you,
with your last eleven years of waves lapping, turning
pages, might like a pretty green pebble in me.
You free the wind inside the water, the aching pulse
that moves the crest, how a song lifts forward
words, waking between the ocean and the sea.

LA GIGANTA

The injured, pitted, pigeon-stained,
diesel-exhausted granite of the gothic cathedral's exterior
soaks up the shadows, yet
the pinks of granite warming early morning,
the pinks in the flower bed,
the pinks of the wings of her illusion,
and the pinks of the dead pigeon
in the plaza of triumph blush.
After all, Our Lady doesn't live far
from the little corner of art.
Professor of faith, she is not troubled
to stand on a symbol of the world.
If she let down her hair,
could you stand the apocalypse?
Her copy exists in her evening shadow
where her favorite couplet is oranges / horses.
Keys, castles, gates, and eagles
have become her decorations,
and her shins are made of lions.
Broken-faced griffins strain to howl water,
and sculptors have chiseled many fires from stone,
but try carrying a bronze sash forever.
Blind as the ecstasy of eye shadow,
she is another name for oceans.
Blue, she suffers for a look, timeless,
something rising to meet her
in a ribbon spiraling, something
like men desperate to see
a city from a tower and live.
You know who to call
if your plow runs into a Roman column
or if you need a human flame for a minaret.
You know a breastplate of righteousness when you see it.
She is lament, proverb, and song
above her bells, above the name of God.

THE RAZOR

What has come to Sevilla but your shoulder's absence
against my chest and a strand of your hair on my sleeve.
Precise is the diamond assault of night on my walk
on the edge of the city where I stand for thresholds.
All I have recorded in my diary of outlandish doors
falls short when I witness one white drape honor the slit
of your summer dress hanging there in the dark
and pristine closet of oblivion. Breezes and years
have passed, so many years in these days; so many faces
like lost marbles and nonsense kings have passed.
From your subtle face, the one I come back to, comes
the breath of love, and it turns the earth casually
like a bracelet of kisses all along the arm of faith
continuing. No one can buy this seductive education
like the practice of a foreign custom, yet I imagine
your face is on the coins of the customs of peace.
Your gaze provokes a ghost behind me in the mirror,
a dissipating weather I can touch after shaving.
I see myself without blood, but the razor, the razor,
the razor of life looms, where you kissed me clean awake
from my dream of freight, my old baby face drawn up
from a well, rescued alive, clean as cold manzanilla.

PENNILESSLY

Honey, we have a little
money. Your old coat might
fight cold, and I know
your lakeside hope can
crystallize like diamonds
held up to old light longing
in prongs of white gold.

Your mind is what the jasmine
buys the wind. A quality the way
the want behind the sunset dying dies.
Might money know the size of time?
We'll never know.

I am a man under moonlight,
who smiles, who walks with a head high
stack of books, now stopping
to put them down and pick up a coin
of moonlight. Which is still a coin
whose only prize is the eyes.
I risk it. I abandon for art's sake
the books like a new altar
as if I could give to God
my love of libraries.
And I do, I pay my payment,
my interest of words
on loan from the dead.

Arise, and let's go north.
The sky roads seem unending.
Disaster may be far, but now
to you I will our memories
of those abandoned birdhouses
in the field above the lake.
We may one day walk there again
picking wild strawberries

enraptured as our children were
that spring practicing with laughter
the disaster plan, clattering
the emergency ladder. And we'll be ready
for the morning of the end of days.

FLOURS

Between geometry and death, she is baking again.
Sisters of the poor, what more can we do
while we wait but breathe, what door
can we build for her courtyard?
To love our country, to bless heaven,
let us build her an outdoor oven.
The sky watches blind as a seed and sees
what will befall us all must rise.

When she reaches up and chooses one flour
over another, loving mothers sigh. The flours
can't imagine what wheat they were
or crumb they may become, so the hours
blink less while she works. They love a little oil.
Who shakes sugar? She does . . . and erases
her labor of white with a labor in white.

We hope she has a crush on us.
She can conceive of that cloud
shaped like a pie rising, raising
its egg-white brushed, burnishing crust
into the blue vault of hunger.

SEVILLA

Sign your name on a hundred tangerines
and leave them around the city. Please, in orange
trees, hang a dozen to mess with children
and nature. Your perfume tastes like windchimes.

Jam and turn the ancient heel of your flamenco
through a concrete block when you are getting on
in years. For now, in the shadow of the bridge to Triana,
where no one has ever pledged love, pledge love.

From libraries, men in suits come for you with tickets.
They are not joking. You have been invited to come
and read old maps while they watch for your hands
that can hold the ten sides of the tower of gold.

The clock on the artillery factory holds fast at 7:30,
and its weather vane of a man with a rifle
is stuck. But your love moves, and before you sleep
and fall into your dreams of storm-chasing, know

the tobacco factory has been turned into a school
where we can learn what rest happens after love.
Still, these buildings anchor history to air. Look
across town. A bullfight escalates into white hankies.

The people want an ear and ears, if possible,
and then they want the weight of death in white
on a chalkboard. They want you to write it,
extending your slender arm and calf.

What are the names of the mysteries?
A ceramic bell. Water without shame.
Lucks, plural. Sword heaven. Candles
on a hat. A peacock in a brass scale.

People believe that judgment comes like a man
dancing behind a whip on the backs of two horses
while the president-of-the-bullfight can only think
of his handkerchief, but these men are more bland

than the palm in your hand. You hold a shield
over the entire city and your belly is full
of the surprising child of poetry. The tourists
and the street-wise circle below, some rising,

some falling like your very DNA, some children,
some horses, some old Basque women beguiling
with rosemary, some lost in the ancient idea of a bit.
Myself, I like your hair up. I like an engine.

A car of fire. A car of earth. A car of water.
A car of common happiness. I would like
to drive you crazy. If you think I will not build
you a house around a box of antique nails,

think again. I will never grow accustomed
to the dance where you kick your own long black skirt.
Your torso demands the sudden striking of palms.
I mean trees. The wood floor hates your brutal shoes.

From your bronze posture, smile down
at our ceilings edged with curves and lit crystals
as we might look at a good white frosting.
Saint of housewives subduing stoves and dragons,

they named a city after your frying pan. Your apron
is a pristine miracle, and your hair pulled back
says you are just about to get serious.
Will you be patient with your knife?

My spine is a sword hidden in your blankets.
Your spine presides over the ministry of air,
and I love your police. Build a museum
on millstones, and curate anchors and tile.

For art has become an advertisement for art
hung from a black cathedral, a scrim like a nighty
for the third largest church in the world
whose pillars weigh so much they are sinking

into the earth, like we all do. Name
some date you want to go horizontal.
History is the building in front of us.
History is a good word in the day of strangers.

History always happens somewhere else
we hope, except when your dress flutters.
For what is a man to a cloud or a mountain,
and when will your eyelash fall on me?

While others fold steel into steel for a month,
sharpen it, and cut the throat of death, we prefer
the triumph of the dead preferring honey
to its nectar youth. We appreciate blood. Come down.

Boats of gold, cocoa, tropical birds, and the future
of smoke will come knots of miles and months fighting
upstream toward one stone tower, but remember
blood is the price and will be the price. Before love,

let's drift like roses, in a river like schools
of freshwater fish, like the blood of six bulls
through the old stone street and into a pipe
on the Guadalquivir all the way to Sanlúcar.

LOVE POEM

Sometimes my shirt makes sparks.
Watch me take it off.

THE PLAZA OF GOOD SUCCESS

Your voice is a poem on fire in a wire birdcage.
It is the black water over which yesterday watches tomorrow.
And the white water over which tomorrow watches yesterday.
When you are quiet, the missing jewel of the finest pendant,
the memory of your voice fills my hair with metal filings,
and each church I pass is a magnet that loves arches.
When I defend my love, your voice sleeps in my ear
like the translucent egg of a wasp.

Where you cry, the shadow of the aqueduct at noon shelters.
Where you sing, we have a more than adequate aqueduct
in which children are racing oranges.

A two-foot fountain falling on itself,
your voice falls like a broken moth,
rises like silver dust from a broken moth.
Your night voice is the bulb, flower and light.
This is the timbre of the last page of a great book.
You whisper promises, and the petals of the almond orchard
shatter. Your words never fill my bones enough,
and this is why I am dying.

At once a naked girl waking
and a woman undressing for bed,
you comfort boys and paralyze men
with hushes. There is no in between.
The mother of worth, great with child,
your feminine power is the God of waves
when you say goodbye. Do you always hum
while you mend torn nets near the ocean?
Your voice doubts safety and saves us
because your voice has big eyes.

Your way of saying things with your hands in a room
angels with its muscles and feathers because it is
the angel of the sun who vacations at the center of the sun.
We know it when we hear the echo

of a woman singing with her eyes closed
who mops concrete steps in an alley
while she thinks of her favorite chapel in a great cathedral.

Praying, you silence the dark that calls itself the light.
You like to say, "the plaza of good success."
There was a yellow-throated bird
one warm winter long ago
who sang to me in a park in Lisbon
where we lay on a blanket outside a museum
near a pond in sunlight while you were silent.

DARK CATHEDRAL

Mornings, you lean against a pillar in a café doorway
near the birthplace of the guitar.
You survey the rocks, a little large, that pave the courtyard,
perfect for a manifestation.
As you breathe through strings, your neck might as well be rosewood.
Any more, we don't think
of a courtyard as a place of justice, but you do. You wash your hands
in a fountain, you brush up
against a rosemary hedge, and you won't take the intricate
and vast interiors for granted.

There is no place like a dark cathedral, and that is why you live there.
You are gothic in the sense
that men should be attacked by butterflies and a viewer should lift his eyes.
You are thoughtful
about the carbon and dust settling on the gold saints. You allow it.
The old Arab bath on the hill
you have turned into a dining room. You develop an economy
of bees for the candle light
no one can resist. Someone looked through your window and said,
With a horseshoe arch
on a horseshoe arch, I will invent a doorway
worthy of her shoulders.

II

What does a rose want?

—Neri Oxman

WITH YOU ASLEEP IN TEXAS

In Spain some say: the streets are not yet paved.
If I were not walking here and standing
and standing and looking so early this morning,
I could occupy a chair of metaphysics.
With whom do I share this view
of a falcon on a bell tower? With you.
You can imagine the feathers and brick.
The white doves of Parque María Luisa
have scattered, and the falcon surveys
the air as confident as the sculptor
who lets light into stone. With you.
The drunk boys stumbling through the streets
love the word *borracho*, rolling the *r*
like a ball down the glass-strewn avenues.
The sloshed girls suffer across the cobbles
in their pumps, have given up on lipstick.
The city gleams like a pinkie-length battery
discarded on a sidewalk settled in a crevice.

My love with the gloves of lavender water,
where are you in your daydream? If I could see you,
I could sketch a study of Eve learning to knit
in lines and to yearn, to turn the thread of the outcast
into the memories of paradise on a blanket
to warm the entire family with a future.

The feeling I wish could last: fear is for others.
I am a traveler who has learned to hush
himself, though my nine smart discourses
on the eight eminent cabinet makers
of Bilbao are in the offing. They took a year off
to make a model province of an old north.
I take my solitary morning walks
to dream about the key of night.
And the world looks through me as if
through a keyhole to the room where you sleep.

Don’t worry over distance any more.
More than death because of faith, our faith,
the targetless arrow has a target.

THE FUTURE OF LOVE

Our bodies
turn us on,
turn on us

like Turner's
skies from seas
turn over

until waves
go whitecap.
Disaster

loves the past
while few love
the future

except for
the dying
who believe

the present
hurting will
un-harden,

find harbor
in the way
a birdcage

on a dock
in shadow
beside a

giant ship
is open
and waiting

not for birds
but for a
museum

and your eyes
which look through
me, see, say:

Let's make love
under an
old black grand

piano
otherwise
known as night.

PASSEIG DE GRÀCIA

Love me like cream cuts coffee. Sharp clouds,
and then the silk throat of a dreamy waking.
Are you obeying me by disobeying oranges,
with olive oil and cinnamon in the thick of salt mist
thinning two miles inland from the sea?

At first, the old man walking below our terrace
with a box the size of himself seems a nobody.
But paint him white and he's a priest of Badalona
come to bless us. He carries beach air in there
and not the sad dust of hospitals some believe.

My delicious sentence, you have the legend
of our map up the sleeve of your sleeveless dress.
The window wants you like a ladder loves a sill.
The color of roe and blood is our flag called Autonomous.
When it waves, I call it kind of drunk on tongues.

Look, the next time we clean fish, we both
hold the knife together, learning spines.
The scales will fly up into a wall of easy beauty
on our arms, and the slit from tail to gills will open
an illusion of jellied June berries in January.

Like peach blossoms at two hundred miles per hour,
I am a joyful small part of your party for color.
What can I do but study your acceleration
and prepare for the impossible test of my life?

POMEGRANATE QUEEN

Not the one with the sash, but the slash.
Phoenicians had their reasons, part origin story
for seasons, part religious myth, and this is partly why
this Christmas I found for you a fruitful grenade,
an apple of a little purse you can pull the pin from
when you want my attention. May I mention
my darkest days are over now? Besides the sky,
my proof is this glossy skin and its yellow-red
of a half-healed bruise—born to crack and be torn back
so we can see the cells the human eye is blind to
in blood blown up. I know you know red's number.

Your grip, your reign, is tougher, tender as an orange
crossed with a life-size heart and an orchard full of
hope-to-die-trying. Color's crucial. Your surreptitious kisses
are richer when you dye your soft lips a gothic red
from those rubies you hide under your tongue.

Show me that lustrous scarlet ribbon hidden
in your mouth as in a Bible marking last things,
for you are more Madonna of the Pomegranate
holding the child holding the fruit holding
the seeds like vermillion bees to be born
from a skull-white honeycomb. How long
will you question the best of what it wants,
your fingertips dipping your nails in crimson?
When done running your tongue among
the slow last of this poem, I don't worry
over those little bits of moist paper you spit
like pretty adjectives, your saliva shining
on them like the pink tint of the winter sun
setting on the Mediterranean off Mojácar.
From mouth to mouth, we might pass the secret
like a clandestine jewel in wartime, each fourteen-carat
garnet kernel, teardrop-tactile honey apple ending
on that wild-cherry-grapeseed bite. Feed me, come

with your 613 laws for love blazing in one heart,
and we will drink. And that intoxicating aftertaste of ink.

ROMANTICISM

In a way, the swallows go through me.
The swallows are swimming over Sevilla,
and from my rooftop I am close enough
to watch one pause between her flapping,
her body an arrow and her gliding wings
that make a drawn bow. She is both
and drawn toward fate by faith.
This afternoon I'll walk to the old town
to find a pen store. I think who sells the ink
and another man who makes it. If he knew you
he would love you, your hair turning silver
more each night of our separation, the silver
men fight for, and your shoulders it touches
the way hunger wants its breakfast bitter
and butter before first light. I'm in the sky,
and I can see a lady preside over the city
from here and how she brings the peace to earth.
I'll wander beneath her skirts in search of even
another pen. I still have my eyes for you
and ears and a hand whose blood can be
a kind of ink in an emergency. Romantic,
I know, and not a metaphor for me.
But that swallow, follow her path home
to rest. Her black loops and cries between
searching and joy, she wrote this poem.

SANTA MARÍA LA BLANCA

Sevilla

Those eyes of mine in 2000 New Hampshire
were ash becoming fire. Then, in the way
the bull ring soil at evening here turns the gold
of a saffron rice, a color began to saturate me.
Like the blood of a statue of an unknown poet,
unreal, my blood had been cool to all my friends,
my family, or even animals, and red to me alone.

For the sake of the singing, my name, and
an attempt at understanding white, I have come
to the orange blossom streets of the virgin
of the good air among the nonsense of dying.
After all, what waits on our horizon is a laying
down, a lying, and a walk of the sad people
who go on worshipping in a church named
Santa María la Blanca whose white waves of ceiling
pastry chefs have tried to imitate in macaroons
and meringues. Though they fail, they win awards
as I did at the altar a year later, standing there
with my windfall bird's nest in one hand
and wild strawberries in the other. At the time
I could imagine like some lame king of Spain:
non plus ultra—nothing beyond—and then
my new world found me like fruit finds a bird.
If love is a walled garden, then in time, sooner
than you think, I am one flower outside climbing
to tear it down with a high, white hello, my tendril
of green want, and the gold stigma of theology
crowning, extending in the air to bees and a queen
my mouth and touch and awe and poverty.

SUBMACHINE GUNS AND HYDRANGEAS

To a fish, there is no such thing as a corner.
To a corner, there is no such thing as a fish.
In her shadow, I falter like a cornered fish.
I stand on a corner sometimes, waiting for a color,
and I am as patient as someone about to meet
a piano, patient as the lover of rivers far
from a river hovering like a bird holding back
above a landing of breadcrumb-strewn concrete.
In the black dress and heels, one woman
from our town deserves an orange suitcase.
She would walk with it as if it were brown,
toy factories shutting down as she passed.
I imagine we travel to an ancient city where we
are protected as dignitaries among terror,
submachine guns, and hydrangeas at the gates.
I know one thing: she has a castle of options.
And I know another: I need a suit of lights.

THE IBERIAN MUSE

Sagres

Virgin of the milk,
you enchant words
and they enchant you.
As I grow older,
leave powdered sugar
on my shoulder
and the smell of wheat
on my neck. Bear with me,
your lonely neighbor
and his cup of nothing.
Even your glance can be
as uselessly pure
as the tongue of a lion
or as wise as a German dwarf genius
to her little princess.

If there is a chime in me,
like a clock-loving queen
find time to wind me at the core.
Tell me to my face the invention
of sifted flour and guitars.
Make a good history of my mistakes.
When I speak here
at the edge of the world
like some plastic bag
tousled in the branches
of a winter-crippled tree,
say, almost almond blossoms.

say, here, it took a brace of mules to turn a key.
Here, the ocean's childhood set sail.
Here with such boredom the Romans executed saints.
Here all that remains of the Moors is almonds.
Some see the nightingale as Mr. Ruin.

Some take the earthquake for a motor.
Some seductive dogs resent a darling.
Some sail and take west for east.

No matter. Your courage to forgive is dangerous adventure.
And you can turn a fig and skinned almonds into a flower.

HOUSEWIFE

When she holds me it is as if
she makes a bed with me in it.

BEDROOM

Like a woman writing Arabic marginalia
around all four sides of an English sonnet
in red ink, kiss my throat in the dark, covering me
fast and slowly like dew lifting at first light.
Before the squash flower of our bed twists closed
trying to hold the memory of a rapt bee,
be thirsty for something in me between my voice
and tongue, perhaps a moan you can translate,
distilling it into the honey of your morning
and a little poison for those who would intrude
on our correspondence with their politics, sports,
and the dull rage of news. Create with me a child
or two and never wake me but define some part of me
in ridiculous terms on behalf of Glossolalia Week.
Grind a lens for squash flower and bee,
and bend over God's idea, jealous as the grave.

TO SLEEP

Like a man in a white suit climbing
the lighthouse stairs, I feel the rail, cold
of a hunger dissipating, winding
and lavendering me, subtly old
like a thick pane that has survived
a century of delinquent boredom.

To sleep, of course close your eyes
and consider all the order
that goes into any white wall,
any stairway loving average steps
no matter how handrail unsteady
or how much museum waits
at its precipice. Heaven's non-stop
is the night when she is here
asleep, also already at the top
of the steep and narrow stair.
The ships are in their chains.
We see them anchored safe
or passing in the lanes.

The gray mist in darkness comes,
and the layers of sheets and cover
deepens, obscuring the vessels,
their intentional drifts and hauls.
And underneath it all, or over,
the pulse of waves, of a light, of blood,
and angels holding swords
ready for the restless jealous that we
might rest and sleep together wholly.

THE HOUSE

That your hands would move across
the stacked stones of my ache like ivy over
the old house so I am suddenly lamplit
and a face at the window profound in its pining.
Not just any ivy, but grapes broad-leafed and soft,
clusters of powdery flesh hidden among the vines
of your yellow-green electricity and tendrils.

My greatest sin is peering into the night as if
you were a house across the street, as if
the thinnest translucent half seashells covered my eyes
on a Monday, when all along you are better
than seaside wine. You know I am anchored,
and your thousands of anchors are what holds.

So falls the hour, each second almost an eyelash,
your each touch just so situated like the lives
of every single flame in fire, calmly leaning
and rising like a wave that swells without falling.

NO DISILLUSION

Flower today, rhetorical vermilion in my throat,
and flutter my attention to the reachable branches.
Each day you open your chemistry of looks I am
a millionaire of moles. I don't want the violence
of a watercolor landscape in mostly silver to mimic
anything more than olive trees reaching
for the horizon on these rolling plains
where the high-speed train you inhabit
is a dream of some rushing lord of arms.
I crave you the way the Spanish love
the olive tree. I nearly hate all others.
Clothes hide you like paint over a painting.
If you were art, I'd pull the great trowel
of my strong forearm across your curves
with almond oil to reveal your colors.
Has no one copied your alabaster
in bronze, or your bronze in alabaster?
I will. I mostly don't believe in ex-angels.
And then you brought the bread and butter.

THE PRETTY

Waiting out my walking pneumonia,
I am sad I could be happy. Propped
in my bed, I moan like a gray horse
left in a downpour outside an old hotel.
My lungs are gray, my cough is gray.
I pray against the water, for the horse
and, delirious, for the unhappy who want more
than anything to step into comic books.
Did I take for granted going out?
Do I take for granted staying in?

Where we can find the pretty, preserved
in olive oil, we can find the winter light
of Andalucía, silver and green
come through a window to white and blue.
Below, past the new patio
of the oldest restaurant in the world,
beyond the collisions of silverware and plates,
listen. Someone is cutting mushrooms.
You do that while everyone openly eats the world,
and the states and governments bus the tables,
or vice versa. Napkins blow down the street
while you stand alone with a blade, unaware
of your sharp posture, yet very aware of swans.
In your kitchen I have waited for you to say,
You just wait.

Like Federico on that kitchen footstool
below his gypsy nursemaid, listening
for another story full of blood and rust
and empty spaces, I will listen to a knife.
I will wait for hunters on the mountain
to come down and appreciate with me
old fire in a passionate kitchen.
If you are near, I am happy I am sad.

A SAIL

Lagos

Pregnant, far, yet weaving closer, she
has come from the smallest white semicolon
of connections to a full-blown answer,
an active sentence in a cornucopia of quiet.
How can a lily petal hold so steady
on a seaside blue plate, and from what
would-be lovers did her lovely covers come?
Women without purses worship her edges
while a storm cloud with a face wonders
into far thunder and the seduction of safety.
The sun on her maritime arms is strong
as the white shirt sleeves of archaeologists.
The finest salt peppers the air.
Some sort of dated stone nautical clock
has the storks clucking and wheeling
to and from their vast high nests.
It is predicting the winds at her back.
Well within her belly there rests cozily
a lunchbox-size mother-of-pearl Eucharist safe
complete with brass lizard lock and a cherub face.
Men standing around small fires,
women and children with your wind compasses,
nation and language of apostrophes and clean seas,
on this sandspit beach, join me
for orange juice and drink the sun's feathers.
We have come around a corner of the world.
Trees walk on water, and promise fills the linen.

MARRIAGE

When you open the door
and step onto the porch for the mail,
a horse has galloped
into a forest.

In the corner, a white wicker rocker
ticks. The world
does not continue exactly.
Where you have been, it shimmers.

You are the blue in the milk of a room.
You are French and long in the eyes
like the shadow of a wire.
You are long for the eyes.

Parrots of light, the paper lanterns hanging
in the window ruffle their colors
with each breeze.

The door, again, and finally,
the sound of the letters turning
in your hand. Beneath your eyes,
the whisper of paper on paper
is like the sheet pulled back
slowly from the bed.

III

They all would find death was quick and marriage
a painful matter.

—*The Odyssey* IV, 346

GRACE

What if rather than a brazen wince and bite,
the mellow fall fruit were to issue from our teeth
into a hand one small apple we hang on a tree

which, in turn, turns into a little pink saying?
If the wet pile of leaves were to push the rake
into our grip and a dry blanket surrounded our feet,

the shattered cornstalk in that field might rise
into silk toward a sun that loved it and then vanish
like a girl playing hide and seek in a long, green sofa.

Watch the squash bugs build a heaven of light
golden roads toward a steady canopy of leaves,
and the brook trout recite mayfly after mayfly.

From behind a long red ribbon and a flourish
of talons, the hawk prestos a living snake.
The hyacinth simply puts on her perfume.

The jade of the daffodil the day before it blossoms
is the yellow for love. Of course the timeless hands
of God cannot hide behind his back that wild garden.

YOUNG WOMAN WITH A SHUTTLECOCK

My everlasting nude
in our museum of innocence,
you have architectural values
and still adore the ruins.
When the earthquake comes,
you know it's OK to lie down
with a fallen chandelier.
I want to tear down signs.
I want to whisper the way
a printing press kisses cotton
a bit over much.
While I'm no cellist,
I like to sit holding you
while you stand leaning
against me, and I do like
horse hair pulled tight
but gentle as reins,
then a music of dark
wine blooming vowels,
old red roses in the nose
wedding science and mystery.

Young woman with a shuttlecock,
you make my poor left hand
love friction's nonfiction.
I am a shepherd of birds.
I am a boy in the woods
who makes a toy from a feather.
I will tell you since you love
the rules: the set continues
even after a fall, flame returned
to your hand by the God of Matches.
Another game begins
in the failing light.
Feathers slow us down.
Feathers will fly.

RELUCTANT LUCK

With just enough sun on a soft black sweater,
she keeps the king standing at a gate
for hours while she wanders, with a book
of poems, at the pace of grazing sheep
El Greco green promontories.
The king is known for his overblown
suit of stone and the horse head
she has convinced him to wear.
Her military is a silver cold front
flying a scabbardfish on its banner.
Hers is a kingdom of sheer cliffs
and sheets, and laundry day signals
a different kind of surrender.
When cold and sunny, she revels
in the solitude of chairs like the queen
of a bakery's late afternoon.
She meditates on an old earthquake,
or the dignity of ungainly storks
who have found poise in a thermal updraft,
or passengers moving inland on a slow train,
or sea snails writing their names and clutching
the dark curves of yuccas in cold weather,
or the joy in the poverty of the farmer's hat.
The masses know her smoke
by its almond oil and lavender,
and her walks favor white stone streets
that wind down to the beaches.
Her favorite toy is a child learning to smell.
She winds her up and lets her go
in a rose garden among hanging,
hand-tatted purses of flower teas.
What is her pet name for passion?
Reluctant luck. How does she entertain
the slow, cold bees of January?
She pours a glass of sherry.

How does she conquer her awe
of the fragrance of lavender?
She steeps it toward a tea.
She steps toward the sea.

BEYOND CÁDIZ

On the television, fields of bleached wheat
and sunflowers by the millions turned
away from the sun. This overwhelming
Andalucían white morning has me back
on a train to the beaches of Cádiz, pondering
the blonde undulations of the land, soil tilled
fresh in long swaths, passing the farmers' fields
and olive orchards, the white stucco towns
fastened together by high tension wires
and dozens of Santa Marías. Speaking of
purity, from the kitchen table I can hear
you turning off the bathwater and then
the quiet of your soaking. I soak it up—
the kitchen chandelier in my spoon
that takes me back to the quotidian clatter
of spoons and dishes in the cafeteria car,
the beautiful woman who fell into our laps
when the train jostled into Jerez.
She joked she hadn't even drunk
her morning sherry yet. A good sport,
she put her hand on your shoulder
and told you, "Fall for this man every time,
don't burn in Cádiz, order the *chipirones*,
and swim out farther than you think
you can go." At least that's what I told you
she told you but she was speaking Catalan,
and I didn't understand a blessèd word
beyond Cádiz.

SONG OF ALMERÍA

The rural bus downshifts to crest a hill and revs,
so a partridge covey flushes into
the lit mist of the late autumn noon, clouds
spilling over higher hills slow and white
like soft glaciers cut by massive stones
the size of fortresses, dissolving into world.

Further on, a goatherd in a great orange sweater
appears like a camouflaged god and staggers
through a rain-soft field where his lithe goats
leap to yet another terrace, headed to the hills,
and I believe he sings. A horizontal pillar
of smoke engulfs him briefly in its trash-fire haze,
and he might make a tragic song of the sea
as he climbs away from the brilliant sea.
He makes believe the mountains lift him.
He goes to prepare a kingdom for me. And you?
I miss you like white smoke misses a clear fire.

SONG OF CATALUNYA

A flag of scarlet saffron strands bleeds gold
into paella. Years of olive oil have seasoned
this pan the patina of any old gold altar
in a poor church. But outside, the blue-green
sea salt thirst breaks patiently mountains
to stone to sand, and anyone sane wants
to start a shell and sea glass jewelry shop.
Here's a gin-blue whale, and there's
a heart of cobalt. A parrot-green parrot
and a beer-brown J so thin and wet it's orange.
This little piece of an old hand-painted plate
still celebrates the porcelain sink it broke in.
With what gold wire can we string it
or hold it in a ring? Gaudí's God was,
in part, a god of stone in, of, for, by
palms. And his tile fired, fractured,
and affixed the way facts can make
a memory. His glass is for light, and ribbons
of bronze guardrails have aged the color
of the wet deer of Andorra. Like Gaudí,
I wish more. More than the Modern.
More than my American subjectivity
are those train cars following one another
into the hills toward Montserrat.
They are like little hand-rolled cigarettes
disappearing into clouds, one after
the other. Up there, enveloped in mist,
in the first of spring, the sycamores praise
with their pruned and crippled limbs
as if that will work. And it does.
Don't wait for hope, fine stranger. Hope
for waiting, confident as the superb eyebrows
of the young woman from Girona
who celebrates a book of poems on the grass
in the park near the zoo by looking away

at nothing and thinking of sepia
while holding the book and holding it.
She holds it unaware of a lion roaring,
unaware of love because she is love
having given herself to poetry. She repeats
to herself: "No good art is not strange.
No good art is not strange."

THE CANNON ON THE RIVER

Late morning I walk out the door,
lock both locks, and a falcon flies over.
Among bus stop cigarettes an hour later
I have already forgotten about fate.
But then the cannon down at the river
concusses over the city its concern
like the darkest of bells rung once,
and you might as well go buy a tomb.
It's only a gunpowder blast that loves
to say its own last name, believes
its place in the history of projectiles.
I'm sure it tries to say power, but this time
only comes a flower of fire and trembling.
Speaking of flour and fire, the old lady
at the bakery is tired of her dusty white life,
no lie, and jokes in English she's ready
to trade the life of her work for opera
and a night life of thorough sleep and dream.
The cannon goes off again and she tells me:
Tell me! so I point to the darkest baguette,
unwhite and unlike all the bread in this town,
brown as a rusted cannon and warm from fire.
I pay and walk through the city with it
under my arm, my warm cannon,
my secret joy darker than any bread
in the province of purity and bone.
I don't even walk home. I head toward
the river that runs days to the ocean,
head toward time, toward the notion
I'll run into someone fantastic—I hope
the man who manned the cannon earlier
this morning will think my bread an omen.
He is not the only one who keeps the secret
of grinding grain to powder, who makes
with force the rising and the heat prevail.

The noon will soon peak like a stamp on a postcard,
ascending like any projectile before its fall.

MOUNTAIN

The mountain must erode
from wind and rain washing away
the soil, plants, and rocks grinding
themselves to dust to make
a fertile valley. And the animals
below who eat the grass and mount
the heights for a change of scenery
or safety, a view, soil, build
with what they carry the mountain
back. Though all comes down,
the wind will carry up feathers
and rain containing particles
of smoke and nitrogen, spider and seed
lift against the wrench of gravity
and death. Sometimes a hundred slaves
will carry the dirt aloft with bags
upon their backs or barrows,
constructing terraces, fighting
the loneliness of sheer rock God
calls up from underground to sky.
Or the devil trying to push a stone
against the sun. Mostly it is made
with solitary molecules in time
blanketing a peak, accreting
for a tree's sake. Years, and on it
a hawk watching. You see,
this tree is like a cross,
and the hawk's talons
are clenched as if nailed there.
And her ancient longsuffering eye,
almost unforgiving, forgives
strangely with a piercing cry.

THE RÍO AGUAS

The steep path to the top of Old Mojácar rises
between the detritus of a decade-old fire, these stacks
of almond branches strewn like war-scorched bodies
and the occasional charred olive stump, between this
high wreckage and the remains of last month's floods
littering the riverbed of the Río Aguas below.
Snail shells bleached all degrees of white litter the trail.
I step past pottery shards strewn among the last vestiges
of the ancient stone walls until I stand atop the hill
before the historic cistern the size of a gasoline tanker.
This cavity of air is half-buried at the top of
the little mountain. Through the gray afternoon
the light wind rises with the trash-fire smoke
from the valley and lifts the cries of parrots
from one of three wealthy, date-palm-bordered estates,
the valley variously terraced with almonds
and olives, figs and pomegranates withering
with the wet days of late fall, and small orange groves
and tangerines. The riverbed winds down from Turre
un-flowing now, full of long stretches of light brown silt,
blonde rocks, torn trees tangled in staggered mounds,
and pooling shallows here and there. Though four days
of rain up north, still nothing coming from the Sierras.
Behind me, two miles or so, the Mediterranean
waits for nothing more than more water and stretches
some darker grays of long lines of waves over gray.
Closer, where the river bed nearly reaches the sea,
in two different silt pits dump trucks remove
load after load of sand from last year's floods.
Cute toy trucks from afar, they must be monstrous
to the workers. A church bell from the town marks
the half hour. Directly below me, one pile of debris
the size of a hotel. A sudden rush of fifty pigeons sweeps by,
some flashing white just a stone's throw away
riding the air up to the stacked white cubes of Mojácar

and gone. I stumble between the flood and fire,
grace in the God's eye view of my God's eye view.

WITHIN

We make another home at the edge
of a city of broken stucco laments,
olives, and orange tree devotion.
Mornings, little men in leather jackets
like black fire hydrants compact
their disillusionments on each corner while
the smallest white dump truck
in the world whines through our streets
with its sunflower of oblivion.
Nights, we shut shutters tight
against the city light.
Tonight we are within
and between a tent of books
on each bedside table beside a river
of sleep rolling away and breaking up
into small pellets like mercury
fallen from a broken thermometer.
We think we hear something stir,
but it is only the wind in a windless city,
rare, of strange value, prophetic.
So, as a white Virgin carried out
of a white church by candlelight
jumps, we jump when our child
bumps the walls with a fever.
In a moment without decisions,
a little flashlight illuminates your arm.

BROOM

To a quiet corner,
you pushed this brush
through dust in a room
to paint nothing but love
in a clean repetition
of shushing sadness.

With a little help,
any old broom curves
away in years, a friction's arc
almost no one measures,
feminine as a deer clear-
ing a fence, a summer
just over, the curve
of your back when you lie in bed
like a flower after a storm.
I measure it.

Away from wind, gold inside
comes home through windows.
The wealth of cleanliness and motes
are in it for the fall's long haul.

THE SWEEPING IN HER ARMS

My wife rakes leaves by the lake
scratching out a song along the shore.
Minuscule grains of sand fly up
so a rare few cling to her shins
like flecks of hair to a long razor.
Even light seems to praise her arms
gentle as any cut wild iris fears
for its own forty-eight-hour flower.
Meanwhile the lapping waves bank
the clarity of coins on her clean sweeps.
Like anything's mortal interest, some want
is in the subtle oil of her palms
leaving warm stains on the handle,
want in the salt of her neck,
want in the sheet of clean-sheet night,
want because she is mine but not mine.
The want is that life goes on without her.

I want to tell the stars to give up—
give up astrology to the presidents
who pile up black sacks of money
for their empty chairs of sentimental friends
and milk the poor with their skeletal cows
who survive in an old contentment
of meat sadness outside Eden.
But all the lowly need now is her look
the way a sidewalk needs a single seed
of cosmos. The poor appreciate green
and the rich are somewhere acting rich
in their white cages while she sweeps who cares.

She sweeps more than leaves and leaves
her mark on order, of order, an open border
like a kitchen ready for a dinner.
She takes a break, leaning on her rake
and thinking the sky mistakes the lake

for its mother, she watches it happen
opening with rain on the distant hills
in the form of a long dress sweeping.

A VISION OUTSIDE THE HOUSE OF THE DUCHESS OF ALBA

Life's a spider dream, and in the web of our city
on a street to a gate inside some sort of fortress
while sparrows flock from one ivy wall
to another, then lifting abruptly up into
the high palm's core like a reverse explosion, below,

here, a servant carries a cup and mothers silence.
She holds it fragile as a speckled egg.
Where I stand watching, the dusk light
shadows of iron bars joke at jailing time.

This is not the time to educate the roses,
rather the modest hour of the lemon blossoms
closing their eyes a little to make a wish
for servants and mothers in the hour of tea.

In my way, I join them and even hope
for an unexpected visit with the Duchess.
A sudden incense from the monastery
is proof enough of a presence
ribboned invisibly across my face.

Believe me. Like a branch of effusive theology,
like the coins of candy from a float,
who is this coming out of the air?

REST

You come across a white hill town in Andalucía
where everyone still believes in television antennas.
You wait in the plaza while the buildings grow whiter.

One day, you walk into one of these buildings
and turn on a television. Nothing happens, but then
a yellow bird throws herself against the window

for a while. You think the reflection must stir up
vanity or jealousy, but the bird only wants a new sky.
Like you. You try, but the window does not open.

The door behind you has a bell on it,
you remind yourself. Your coming and going
is a music, and that's the way it should be.

The seeds in the sunflower fields will soon be ready.
Between the black, the white in them is the white
of buildings and the white of bones. Ask yourself

if the kitchen cupboard cries for oil or solitude.
Once, rooms were anointed and the smallest splatters
became reminders of belief. Stain the bedroom

with your scent. And give your shadow sheets.
Find the bed whose pillow is always cool.
For sleep no lithe sheep should be needed.

Your kiss can pickpocket the pickpocket.
The confidence of a small bronze bell
on a giant wooden door is the meaning of rest.

Acknowledgments

I am grateful to the magazine editors who first published the various poems in this collection:

Arkansas International, Birmingham Poetry Review, Colorado Review, Copper Nickel, The Common, Five Points, Hayden's Ferry Review, Hobart, Image, Ink & Letters, McNeese Review, Meridian, Mumber Magazine, New England Review, Passages North, Prairie Schooner, Prelude, Quarterly West, Southern Indiana Review, Southern Review, Sou'wester, Spillway, Subtropics, Swing, Terrain.org, Thrush, Times Literary Supplement, Tuesday (An Art Project), Valparaiso Poetry Review

Virginia Center for the Creative Arts provided a generous residency, allowing me time and space and solitude to revise these poems.

This book was set in ITC Galliard, designed by Matthew Carter and published in 1978. It is based on the sixteenth-century type created by Robert Granjon. The name Galliard refers to a lively dance of that era and Carter's type has long been admired for both its energy and elegance. It is perhaps best known for its "pelican-beak" italic letter "*g*."

This book was designed by Shannon Carter, Ian Creeger, and Gregory Wolfe. It was published in hardcover, paperback, and electronic formats by Slant Books, Seattle, Washington.

Cover photo by Sven Birkerts.
Used by permission.

www.ingramcontent.com/pod-product-compliance
Lightning Source LLC
LaVergne TN
LVHW051019080826
845145LV00009B/2709

9781639822119